# M551 Sheridan in action

By Jim Mesko
Color By Don Greer
Illustrated by Joe Sewell

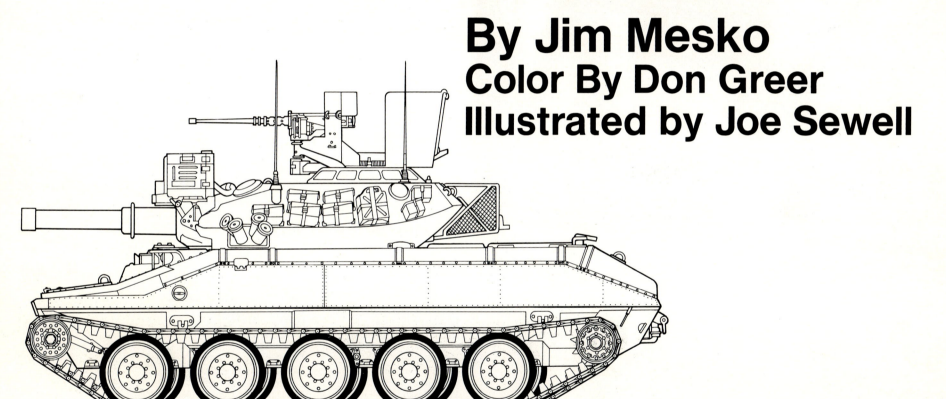

Armor Number 28
squadron/signal publications

***CLOUD NINE***, an M551 Sheridan of the 3rd Squadron, 11th Armored Cavalry Regiment fords a stream under fire near the Cambodian border during 1969.

COPYRIGHT © 1990 SQUADRON/SIGNAL PUBLICATIONS, INC.
1115 CROWLEY DRIVE   CARROLLTON, TEXAS 75011-5010
All rights reserved. No part of this publication may be reproduced, stored in a retrieval system or transmitted in any form by any means electrical, mechanical or otherwise, without written permission of the publisher.

ISBN 0-89747-253-5

If you have any photographs of the aircraft, armor, soldiers or ships of any nation, particularly wartime snapshots, why not share them with us and help make Squadron/Signal's books all the more interesting and complete in the future. Any photograph sent to us will be copied and the original returned. The donor will be fully credited for any photos used. Please send them to:

Squadron/Signal Publications, Inc.
1115 Crowley Drive.
Carrollton, TX 75011-5010.

# Dedication

In Memory of "Bonz" and to the men and women of the U.S. Army Armor Force.

# Acknowledgements

| | |
|---|---|
| U.S. Army | U.S. Air Force |
| Patton Armor Museum (PAM) | Armor Magazine |
| Fort Knox PAO | PAO, 82nd Airborne Division |
| LCOL Gordon Kurtz | LCOL John Calior |
| LT Mark Osterhage | SGT Deidre Cozzens |
| Captain Jeffrey Erickson | Mike Green |
| Greg Stuart | Dana Bell |
| Pete Harlem | D. Schmidt |
| Richard Hunnicutt | 2nd Training Brigade, E Troops, |
| Stella Mesko | (OPFOR) |
| Peter Mesko | Nat'l. Training Center Headquarters, |
| Ron Mihalenko | 3rd Battalion, 73rd Armor, 82nd |
| | Airborne Division |

***HARD CORE***, an M551 Sheridan of the 3rd Squadron, 4th Cavalry, assigned to the 25th Infantry Division, moves through light jungle during February of 1969. This unit was one of two equipped with the Sheridan as part of the vehicle's Vietnam combat test. The frame and wire on the front was a field modification designed to detonate RPG rounds before they hit the vehicle. (USA)

# INTRODUCTION

Although the Army was generally satisfied with the M41 Walker Bulldog tank, it was decided during late 1952 to begin development of a new vehicle to fill an Army requirement for an air transportable/deployable light tank. While the M41 was capable of being carried by existing transport aircraft, it was not capable of being dropped by parachute.

The Korean War had underscored the need for the Army to be able to rapidly deploy forces to trouble spots on a moments notice. To meet this requirement, a lighter, smaller tank that could be airlifted into combat was needed. While efforts were made late in the M41's production run to upgrade its armament, nothing could be done to reduce its overall weight and size. This led to the Army's decision to develop a totally new vehicle.

The first vehicle the Army examined was a proposal from Cadillac, designated the T71. Armed with a 76MM cannon, this design was smaller, lighter and less expensive than the Bulldog. Lightly armored, the T71 had a relatively conventional layout. In the event, the Army decided not to issue a production contact.

Instead, the Army decided to develop a design submitted by AAI, Incorporated, designated the T92. This vehicle, unlike the T71, did not follow conventional light tank design. The 76MM cannon was mounted far back on the hull between two small machine gun turrets and was not enclosed within an armored turret, as on a conventional tank. Although lightly armored, which resulted in a substantial drop in weight when compared to the M41, the slope of the hull was such that it offered excellent ballistic protection. Development of this unconventional design began during 1954, with prototype trials starting during 1957. While the basic vehicle proved to be acceptable, the Army realized that its main armament was incapable of dealing with the next generation of Russian armor (such as the T54/T55 series). A study was done to see if the T92 could be rearmed with a 90MM cannon; however, it was determined that the chassis could not handle the extra weight. As a result, the Army decided not to put the T92 into production.

With the realization that the 76MM cannon could no longer cope with the newer Soviet tanks, the Army had a serious problem. While it needed an air transportable/deployable light tank with an armament capable of handling potential opponents, the two requirements proved to be incompatible. If the tank was to be capable of being dropped by parachute, it had to be fairly light. If it was to be able to deal with current Soviet armor, it had to carry a larger gun, which meant a fairly heavy chassis. There seemed to be little possibility of developing a light tank which could carry a gun capable of knocking out anticipated adversaries, while remaining parachute deployable. At the same time, the Army hoped that if such a vehicle could be developed, it could also be employed by armored cavalry units for screening and reconnaissance.

At this critical point, plans for a revolutionary new weapons system was being studied by the Army. This new system envisioned using a combination gun/missile launcher which would do away with the conventional rifled gun tube and heavy recoil system. The key to the system was the relatively light missile launcher unit which would enable the vehicle to carry a significantly larger armament than would be possible with a similar caliber conventional gun. The missile's range and penetration capability would be superior to the existing guns on other medium tanks.

The Army decided that if the system, code named *Shillelagh*, passed all its development tests and worked properly, it would be incorporated on a new light tank, a version of the current M60, and in the MBT-70, a new main battle tank under consideration. In addition to the missile, the gun/launcher was also capable of firing caseless (i.e. combustible) rounds.

Designated the Armored Reconnaissance/Airborne Assault Vehicle, the Army requested proposals from various companies for the project. A number of firms tendered replies and, from the various proposals, the General Motors (GM) design was selected for development during the Spring of 1960. Given the designation XM551, a contract for six prototypes was issued and GM began work on these immediately. Plans for the

**The standard Army light tank during the 1950s was the M41 Walker Bulldog. Although a fine vehicle armed with a 76MM cannon, the M41 could not be air-dropped, a feature the Army wanted for its next light tank. (PAM)**

**One of the vehicles the Army studied as an M41 replacement was the T92 from AAI, Incorporated. The T92 was a radical design, being low and angular. It mounted as its main armament a 76MM cannon in a turret mounted far back on the hull. It also had two smaller machine gun turrets on either side of the main turret. (PAM)**

finalized vehicle were approved in December of 1961, coinciding with the trials of the first automotive test vehicle. Additionally, the Shillelagh missile system had begun its full scale evaluation, being mounted in a special test bed turret, fitted to an M41 hull.

Although six prototypes had originally been authorized, the Army decided to purchase an additional six test vehicles for an extensive test program. These prototypes bore little resemblance to the actual production vehicle, having a box type hull and different road wheels. Additionally, there was no flotation screen installed on the prototypes. The prototypes were put through numerous trials to test for endurance, climate adaptability, amphibious characteristics, firing characteristics and airborne delivery. Although numerous problems arose, these were to be expected with such a radical design.

Most of the automotive problems were solved fairly easily; however, the main difficulty was with the Shillelagh gun/missile system. While the development of the missile round went relatively smoothly, the conventional high explosive (HE) ammunition caused a great many problems. Since the Shillelagh system was also intended for use on the MBT-70 tank, which was to be completely sealed for protection under Nuclear, Biological, and Chemical (NBC) battlefield conditions, the HE rounds were designed to have almost totally combustible casings, eliminating the need to get rid of the bulky spent casings. With the combustible casing, only a small brass firing end piece was left.

While in theory this sounded fine, in actual practice the combustible casing was often not completely consumed. The major reason for this was that the combustible case absorbed moisture from the humidity in the air and this moisture was just enough to stop consumption of the complete round. The residue left in the barrel was hot enough to occasionally ignite the next round when it was chambered — with disastrous results. Additionally, the rounds occasionally absorbed so much moisture that the case distorted to the point that the round could not be chambered.

In spite of these problems which would have eventually been solved with more testing, certain factions within the Army (who were responsible for tank procurement) pushed for the XM-551 to be placed in production. Another faction, representing the field users, wanted the bugs worked out before the vehicle was placed into production; in that way it would be fully operational when issued to the troops.

Unfortunately, the first group had their way and, during mid-1965, a four year contract was issued to GM's Allison Motor Car Division for the vehicle, under the designation M551 General Sheridan. The decision to rush the vehicle into production before its various problems were solved would later prove to be a serious mistake and would eventually cause disastrous consequences for future American tank development.

**In comparison to the M41 Walker Bulldog, the T92 was much lower and weighed substantially less. The low, angular design offered much better ballistic protection for the amount of armor carried than a more conventional hull design. (PAM)**

**During the early 1960s, a breakthrough in weapons development offered the Army a light weight, high-powered, combination gun/missile system which did away with the need for a heavy recoil system. The end result of this research was the XM551 Sheridan. This is one of the early research and development vehicles. (PAM)**

# Development

**Prototype XM551**

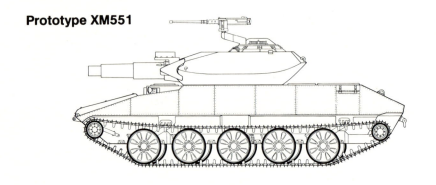

**M551 (Early)**

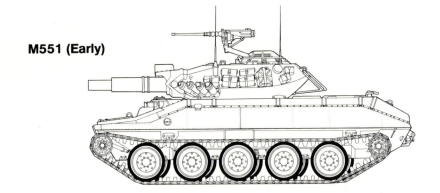

**M551 (Late)**

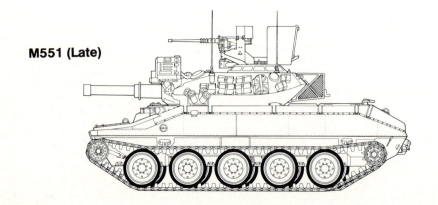

**Sheridan/T-72**

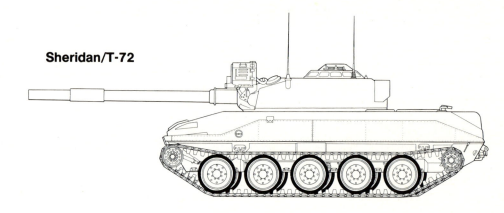

**Sheridan/BMP**

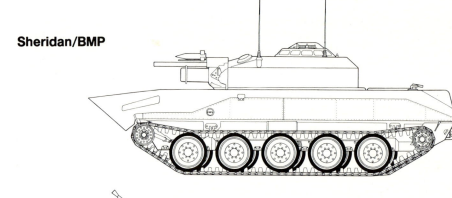

**Sheridan/ZSU-23-4**

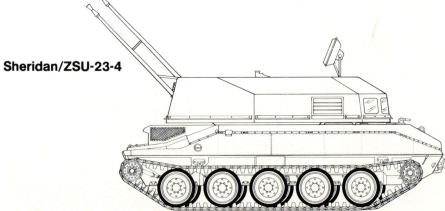

# M551 Sheridan

The production M551 Sheridan, which began coming off the assembly line during 1965, bore little similarity to the twelve prototype/test vehicles. The production vehicle had replaced the box like hull structure with a far more angular shape for better ballistic protection. The hull, comprised of welded aluminum armor, was divided into three compartments. The front compartment housed the vehicle's driver, the middle served as the fighting compartment, and the rear compartment housed the engine.

The driver had an unusual hatch which, when opened, pivoted 180° to the rear, coming to rest inside the hull. Vision, with the hatch closed, was supplied by three periscopes, with the center periscope being capable of taking an infrared lens for night driving. The fighting compartment housed the turret basket, extra ammunition and various other incidental equipment.

Power for the Sheridan was provided by a 3,000 horsepower V6 water-cooled turbocharged diesel engine, which was coupled to a six speed transmission (four forward, two reverse gears). This engine provided a high horsepower to weight ratio due to the M551's light weight, giving the vehicle a top speed of forty miles per hour. The internal fuel tank (at the rear) held some 160 gallons of diesel fuel, giving the M551 a range of 375 miles. The engine compartment had a fire extinguisher system which could be activated by the driver, or from the outside by pulling a handle on the port side of the hull above the first two road wheels.

The suspension system consisted of five road wheels mounted on a torsion bar suspension with the drive sprocket situated in the rear and the idler wheel in the front. No track return rollers were fitted and the first and last road wheels were fitted with hydraulic shock absorbers.

The turret, mounted above the center fighting compartment, was constructed of welded steel armor. Two hatches were provided: one on the starboard side for the tank commander (TC) and one for the loader on the port side. The TC's hatch was set in a cupola fitted with ten vision blocks for 360° coverage. Mounted on the cupola was a gun mount for a .50 caliber M2 machine gun. One problem area was that, when using the .50 caliber machine gun, the commander was fully exposed to enemy fire. This fact later led to the development of an armored "crows nest" for use in Vietnam.

The loader was provided with an M37 periscope, which could rotate 360°, mounted just in front of his hatch. The gunner was seated on the starboard side of the hull below the TC, with an M129 telescope sight coupled to the main gun. For night firing, he had an infrared M44 sight mounted on the turret roof. When using the missile system, the gunner would guide the round to the target by keeping the target aligned in the cross bars of the sight. Changes in the missile's course were automatically adjusted by signals sent

**The production Sheridan differed greatly from the prototype. The boxy hull was replaced by a more tapered design with new road wheels and flotation gear. Due to problems with burning residue left in the barrel by the combustible casing ammunition, an open breech scavanger system was installed to clear it. (USA)**

from the tank to a small infrared tracker mounted in the tail of the missile. Unfortunately, the missile had a dead zone under 1,000 meters during which it was ineffective.

Conventional rounds required no such guidance and were fired in a normal manner. Originally, only a high explosive round was designed for use in the gun, but events in Vietnam later led to the development of a cannister or "Beehive" round. Additionally, white phosphorus and training rounds were also made for use with the Sheridan. The Sheridan also mounted a coaxial 7.62MM machine gun. A normal ammunition load for the M551 consisted of twenty conventional rounds, eight Shillelagh missiles and basic machine gun ammunition loads for the .50 caliber and 7.62MM machine guns.

The Sheridan was originally supposed to be fully amphibious, much like the Russian PT-76; however, this requirement was modified as the vehicle progressed from the prototype stage into production. Eventually, a flotation screen was incorporated into the design which was erected around the top of the hull from storage points along the hull outer edge. It took between five to ten minutes to set up the screen. When complete, the vehicle was enclosed in the canvas screen except in the front where a flotation plate provided a rigid surface to push aside choppy water. This system was intended primarily for use in river crossings and could not be used for an amphibious landing. Propulsion in the water was provided by the Sheridan's tracks, which were also used to steer the vehicle.

The M551 was capable of being air dropped by parachute. While this was a useful characteristic, it was seldom used because of the numerous problems which could arise if there was a failure of any of the parachutes, or if they did not open at the same time. Instead, a maneuver called the Low Altitude Parachute Extraction System (LAPES) is normally used to get the vehicle onto the ground when a usable runway is not available. In this maneuver, the transport aircraft (normally a Lockheed C-130 Hercules) makes a low pass over the landing zone (LZ) and at the appropriate moment a drogue parachute is released, which opens the main parachutes and pulls the tank (strapped down to a pallet) out the rear of the aircraft. The pallet absorbs most of the landing impact and the vehicle's crew (who parachuted in separately) then releases the lines securing it to the pallet and drives it into action.

As with other modern American AFVs; the Sheridan is equipped with an NBC system to protect the crew. The crew is well provided with vision ports and for night fighting, the tank commander, gunner and loader all have infrared sights and viewing equipment. Additionally an infrared searchlight was retrofitted to the turret alongside the 152MM gun on the port side. Smoke grenade launchers were also fitted to the underside of the forward portion of the turret to provide cover.

Initially a small rack was mounted on the turret rear for personal storage. This was later replaced by a number of field installed larger racks in Vietnam which greatly increased what could be carried outside the vehicle. These unofficial racks never became standard issue and most Sheridans retained the original rack throughout their service life. Provisions were made for carrying extra machine gun ammunition boxes externally on the turret sides, as well as jerry cans for fuel, oil or water.

The driver of the M551 was positioned in the center of the hull behind a rather unusual hatch. The hatch rotated 180° to open and was equipped with three vision periscopes. The center periscope could be fitted with an infrared lens for night driving. (Mesko)

## Hull Development

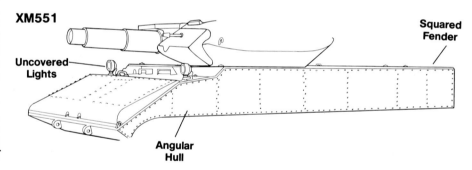

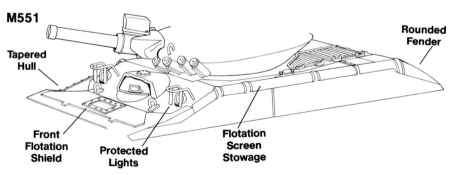

The turret had two hatches, one for the tank commander (on the starboard side) and another for the loader (on the port side). While the commander had a series of vision blocks for all-round visibility, the loader had a periscope, which could rotate 360°, mounted directly in front of his hatch. (Mesko)

## Road Wheels

XM551

M551

The Sheridan was designed to be amphibious through the use of raised canvas flotation screens. This early production vehicle, fitted with a 76mm cannon, has the screens raised as part of a demonstration of the vehicle during 1967 at the Rock Island Arsenal. (PAM)

The commander's hatch was fitted with a mount for a .50 caliber machine gun. The split hatch covers raised vertically to provide a small degree of protection for the commander when firing the gun. This was found to be inadequate and a special set of shields was designed to fit around the hatch for additional protection. (Mesko)

An M551 Sheridan comes out of the water during tests of its flotation screen. The rigid front screen was known as the "surfboard" and was fitted to the front top of the forward hull. Once erected, the rigid screen allowed the Sheridan to move through the water at a good pace. (PAM)

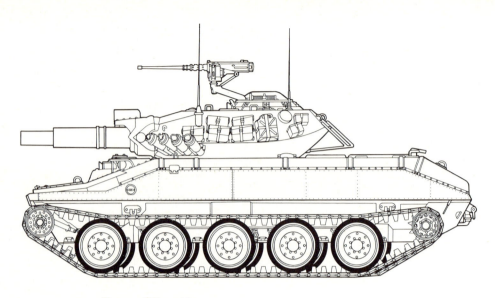
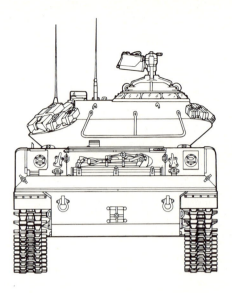

## Specifications

# M551 Sheridan

| | |
|---|---|
| Crew | Four |
| Length | 20.43 Feet |
| Width | 9.25 Feet |
| Height | 9.66 Feet |
| Weight | 34,899 Pounds |

**Armament**
| | |
|---|---|
| Main | 152mm gun/missile launcher. |
| Secondary | One 7.62mm coaxial machine gun. One .50 caliber M2 Browning on commander's cupola. |
| Engine | Detroit-Diesel 6V-53T 300 hp turbocharged diesel engine. |
| Speed | 43.5 mph |
| Range | 373 miles |

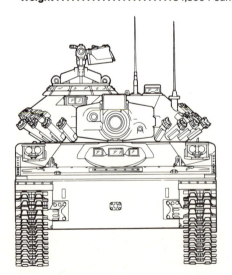
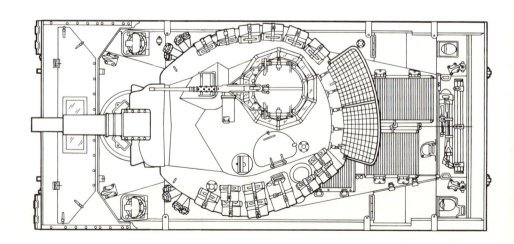

Access to the Sheridan's engine compartment is gained by raising the two engine grilles and removing the rear hatch cover. The battery compartment is located just under the raised grille (top). (Mesko)

This removed Sheridan powerplant rests on a dolly which allows it to be easily moved by maintenance personnel. The transmission is painted White, as is the coolant surge tank. (Mesko)

The radiator cooler fan is visible just behind the White painted radiator housing (right). The spring located just to the left of it is the belt tensioner for the generator coolant fan belts. These belts had caused problems in early Sheridans before they were strengthened. (Mesko)

This C-130 Transport in making a Low Altitude Parachute Extraction pass over the landing zone. The parachute is dragging the pallet from the rear of the aircraft as it flies a very low and slow pass. (USA)

A Sheridan, on it's pallet, is pulled from the rear of a C-130 making a LAPES run on an LZ. The pallet will cushion the landing of the vehicle. (USA)

The pallet and Sheridan skid to a stop behind the C-130 that dropped them. Once the vehicle is safely on the ground the crew will disconnect it from the delivery pallet and drive it off. (USA)

The Sheridan can also be delivered into a landing zone (LZ) by parachute. Because of the problems associated with dropping large cargos, this method is rarely used. (USA)

The most serious problem with the Sheridan was in the combustible case ammunition, while the development of the missile round went smoother. The missile gave the Sheridan tremendous fire-power and could kill a target at a range of 4,000 meters. This M551 has just fired a missile round during testing. (PAM)

Normally, the combustible round did not totally consume itself and dangerous residue was left in the barrel which could ignite the next round chambered. To help clear the barrel an open breech scavenger system was fitted to the gun tube. These vehicles, such as this one being tested by the Test and Evaluation Command, could be identified by the large cylinder around the barrel. (PAM)

An early production Sheridan undergoes field trials conducted by the Armor Board at Fort Knox during 1965. Mechanically the Sheridan also experienced problems, which was not unusual for a new vehicle. The decision to rush the vehicle into production before these problems were solved led to further problems for field units. (USA)

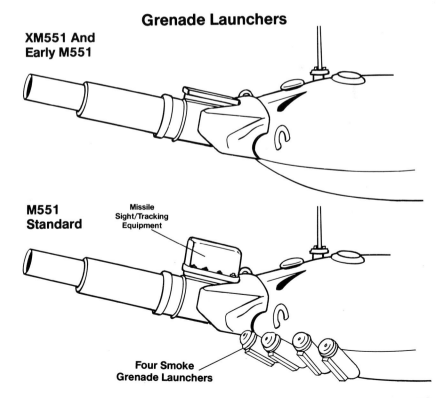

# Into Service

When the M551 Sheridan was introduced into service it still had numerous technical problems which had to be solved. While the representatives from the various field units wanted these problems corrected before the M551 was issued to Armor troops in the field, the various agencies responsible for its development pushed for a quick service introduction, promising that the defects would be quickly rectified.

The major problem with the Sheridan centered around its armament. While there were some problems with the missile, these were not unexpected. The problems were relatively minor when compared to those experienced with the combustible casing rounds. This ammunition still had problems with incomplete combustion and case distortion due to humidity absorption. A number of chemical coatings were tried on the casing to lessen its susceptibility to moisture but none proved totally effective. A plastic bag was then designed which fit snugly around the ammunition to keep out moisture. This proved more effective, but did not totally eliminate the problem.

Unable to satisfactorily solve the ammunition problem, the Army decided to equip the gun with an open-breech scavenger system. This system forced air into the barrel in order to clear away any burning residue. Unfortunately, this open breech system allowed the residue, smoke and carbon monoxide to be blown back into the turret. The burning residue posed the most serious problem, since there was a good possibility that it could ignite ready rounds. The smoke hindered crew operations and the carbon monoxide quickly built up to dangerous levels.

The scavenger system was introduced into production vehicles during early 1967. Despite the problems with the system, it was not discontinued on the production line until later that year. It was then replaced by a closed breech scavenger system (CBSS) which was introduced during early 1968. The CBSS blew the debris out the barrel while the breech remained closed, preventing the residue, smoke and fumes from entering the turret. This system proved highly effective in reducing many of the problems associated with the combustible case ammunition, but it experienced numerous mechanical problems which often rendered it inoperable. Externally, the two systems were distinguished by the large tube around the gun barrel, which identified vehicles with the open breech system.

When the Sheridan was first considered for production, the vehicle was intended to operate in a European type conventional war situation. When the Sheridan finally went into production, however, the U.S. was heavily involved in a guerrilla war in South Vietnam. In anticipation of possible deployment to the war zone, a production vehicle was field tested in Panama to determine how the vehicle would function in a jungle environment.

Aside from the ammunition moisture problems which were worse in the jungle, these tests revealed numerous deficiencies in the basic M551 chassis. Engine overheating was common, engine noise was excessive and the recoil system and firing circuit often malfunctioned. Additionally the missile round proved highly unreliable, prompting the Army to consider a new gun system (this was later dropped). A metal casing was considered to solve the problems with the combustible round, but this idea was also dropped when it became evident that this type of round was incompatible with the new MBT-70 under development.

Additional tests were also conducted on the M551 in Alaska, by the Australian Army under jungle conditions, and in Great Britain. In each case the results were disturbing. Due to a variety of problems uncovered during cold weather testing, a recommendation was forwarded to the Pentagon against deploying the Sheridan under conditions of extreme cold. The Australians uncovered many of the same problems which had surfaced during the Panama trials, along with other deficiencies concerning the conventional round (its range) and problems with the gunner's sighting system.

In rejecting the Sheridan for use by its forces, the Australian Army pointedly remarked that it would be unsuitable for a counter-insurgency type war, like that going on in Vietnam, which was the only type of conflict in which Australian forces would be involved in the near future. Great Britain also found fault with the Sheridan and did not pursue the purchase of the vehicle.

Despite the problems with the vehicle, it was decided to send the Sheridan to U.S. Forces in Vietnam as a field test.

**One of the first units to receive the M551 Sheridan was the Armor Training Command at Fort Knox. These vehicles were used for training tank crews for operational assignment to units using the vehicle. These early production M551s were fitted with the open breech scavenger system. (Mihalenko)**

Problems with the Shillelagh gun/launcher armament led to the Sheridan being fitted with a number of different weapons to test the feasibility of rearming the vehicle. This Sheridan at the Rock Island Arsenal has been fitted with the same 76MM cannon used on the M41 Walker Bulldog.

A Sheridan from the 4/9 Cavalry crosses a river with the flotation screen deployed during training maneuvers. The hull markings are in White. The 4/9th Cavalry was one of the first field units to receive the Sheridan. (PAM)

One of the first units to receive the M551 Sheridan in Vietnam was the 1st Squadron, 11th Armored Cavalry. Tankers from the unit prepare their vehicles for combat operations at their home base of Xuan Loc. (Mihalenko)

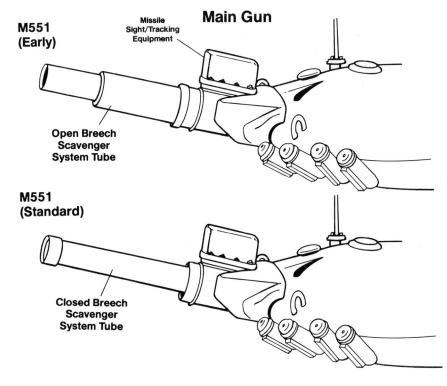

**Main Gun**

M551 (Early) — Missile Sight/Tracking Equipment, Open Breech Scavenger System Tube

M551 (Standard) — Closed Breech Scavenger System Tube

# Vietnam

The numerous problems which plagued the Sheridan caused serious criticism of the program both by Congress, which was becoming increasingly anti-military due to the Vietnam War, and by certain groups within the Army itself. These groups questioned the rationale and high cost of the entire program. The developmental agencies responsible for rushing the Sheridan into production before all the problems were corrected were caught between the proverbial "rock and a hard place." They had to do something to show that the M551 was a viable weapons system and that their earlier decision had been correct. They decided to push for the introduction of the Sheridan into combat in Vietnam. Here they hoped that it would prove itself on the battlefield and silence their critics.

The problems with the Sheridan program were common knowledge and U.S. field commanders in Vietnam were opposed to the deployment of the M551 for widespread use in the war. This opposition was in part due to the fact that no anti-personnel round existed for use with the main gun. This was a serious problem since the expensive anti-tank round would be worthless in Vietnam and the high explosive (HE) round offered no upgrade in firepower over the 90MM gun used on the M48A3 Patton.

The development of an anti-personnel round, the M6252 Canister or "Beehive" round solved the problem. This shell, containing nearly 10,000 steel flechettes (small dart-shaped projectiles), gave the Sheridan an anti-personnel round which could be devastating against troops in the open or under light cover. With this round the 152MM gun became a huge shotgun.

As a result of this development, sixty-four Sheridans were cleared for deployment to Vietnam during early January of 1969. Originally it was planned to equip two divisional cavalry squadrons with M551s. This was changed after COL George S. Patton suggested to the U.S. Commander in Vietnam, GEN Creighton Abrams, that a fairer test program would result from assigning the Sheridan to both a divisional cavalry squadron and a regimental squadron. As a result, the M551s were assigned to the 3rd Squadron, Forth Cavalry and the 1st Squadron, 11th Armored Cavalry Regiment (Blackhorse Regiment). Each unit received twenty-seven vehicles, the 3rd exchanging their M48A3 Pattons on a one for one basis, while the 1st exchanged two M113 ACAVs for three Sheridans. Therefore, one unit exchanged a heavier, more capable vehicle (M48) for the more lightly armored M551, while the other received a more heavily armored and armed vehicle in place of the lighter ACAV.

When the Sheridans arrived in Vietnam they were accompanied by factory tech reps, instructors and evaluators to assist each unit in their transition to the M551. Each unit, however, decided to approach the transition in a different way. While the 11th ACR stood down an entire troop for seven days of uninterrupted training, the 3rd/4th Cavalry decided to train while still maintaining operations. As a result, the 11th ACR troops learned much more during their training period, while the 3rd/4th Cavalry personnel were often absent from the training briefs because of other commitments, which had a serious affect on their smooth transition to the vehicle. Both units, however, were ready to start combat operations with the Sheridan by early February.

From the outset the M551's employment by the 3/4th Cavalry did not go well. The unit did not want to exchange their trusted M48 Pattons for the less capable Sheridan and many felt the vehicle was being forced on them by Army higher ups. This already negative attitude was reinforced by the first combat test of the vehicle. A Sheridan triggered a twenty-five pound pressure detonated mine which ruptured the hull. The resulting fire ignited the caseless ammunition and led to the complete destruction of the M551 and the death of the driver.

This experience made the crews exceptionally "gun shy", since a similar mine would have only blown off a road wheel or two on an M48. The ACAV would have probably been severely damaged; however, with the ACAV there would have been no secondary explosion and only minor crew injuries. This inauspicious start to Sheridan operations colored the view of the men of the 3/4 Cavalry and other units soon picked up on this.

A month later, on 10 March, the unit's confidence in the vehicle received a much needed shot in the arm. While in the field near Tay Ninh City, a night observation post reported enemy movement in an open field near the Ben Cui Rubber Plantation. Sheridan crews from Troop A spotted a large group of NVA by using their night observation devices. Reacting quickly, the crews fired a number of "Beehive" rounds which cut a swath through the enemy troops. Taken by surprise and devastated by the firepower being used against them, the NVA milled around in confusion, then broke and ran. The fleeing enemy left over forty dead behind, killed by the Sheridan's firepower. Although this action did much to increase the confidence in the Sheridan, there still was doubt among individual soldiers about its ability to withstand battle damage from mines and rocket propelled grenades (RPGs).

By comparison, the 11th ACR's deployment of the vehicle went fairly smoothly. The uninterrupted week of training gave the crews confidence in their ability to operate with the Sheridan. Additionally the fact that they were gaining a vehicle which had considerable more firepower than their older M113 ACAVs made them more willing to accept the M551. Their first combat further instilled confidence in the vehicle. Two troops, A and B,

**The 3/4th Cavalry, based at Cu Chi, normally carried large numbers on the sides of the hull in White and a colored band around the gun to denote different troops. This M-551 of B Troop has a White band around the barrel and a Yellow Knight's chess head further back on the barrel. (Schmidt via Harlem)**

of the 1st Squadron were moved to Bien Hoa during early February as a quick reaction force to counter an anticipated enemy offensive. Code named *Task Force Privette* (after its commader) the unit was mortared on 23 February and moved out in search of the enemy. Almost immediately, a mixed VC/NVA force was engaged and Privette quickly moved the two troops of Sheridans on line and they began to fire canister rounds at the enemy. The devastating fire of the 152MM Beehive rounds caused panic among the communist ranks and they broke and fled, leaving behind over eighty dead.

The Sheridan's initial test period ran for three months and ended in May. Each unit's evaluation of the Sheridan varied, partially because of preconceived ideas, initial training and a comparison with the vehicle it had replaced. Both, however, pointed out many of the same problems which had turned up in the Panama trials and by the Australians. Additionally, being engaged in field operations cut down on maintenance time, which was further compounded by a lack of spare parts and qualified maintenance facilities. In particular, the humid Vietnamese climate played havoc with the electrical system, which also proved highly susceptible to dust and excessive vehicle vibration. Another major problem was engine overheating. This was traced to faulty fanbelts and aluminum pullies, which constantly broke (which also led to a loss of electrical power). Eventually this problem was solved by the use of stronger fanbelts and steel pullies.

The two worst problems, however, were the Sheridan's inability to withstand mines and RPG hits and the combustible case ammunition. The vehicle, because of its light weight, could not take the punishment that the M48 could and the crews quickly learned to abandon the vehicle when it was hit, for fear of a secondary explosion. The explosion was caused by the rupture of the combustible rounds, a problem which the crews of the M48 Patton never had to worry about. A partial solution was the installation of titanium armor panels under the bow which helped reduce the risk from mines. There was, however, no available solution to combat the RPG problem. In all fairness, the Sheridan had never been designed to stand up to the kind of punishment an M48 could take, but its armor protection was not as good as it had been initially hoped.

As for the combustible rounds, this was probably the single greatest concern put forth by the crews. Its susceptibly to moisture, inability to take rough handling, along with the quickness with which the rounds ruptured and detonated after the vehicle had been hit were major concerns. Even the plastic bag developed to protect the rounds did little good, since many crews stripped them off prior to combat so that they would be ready at a moments notice in a combat situation.

Despite these problems, the Army decided to send more Sheridans to Vietnam. These vehicles would have some of the changes required to correct some of the more glaring deficiencies in the vehicle. This decision was made primarily because of the more optimistic recommendations of the 11th ACAR, which felt that the Sheridan was superior overall to the M113 ACAV, particularly in firepower. The developmental agencies grabbed at this chance to vindicate themselves and by 1970 over 200 Sheridans were in Vietnam equipping almost all of the cavalry units in-country.

The Sheridans served until the final withdrawal of American forces with mixed results. New fan belts and pullies helped solve the engine overheating problems, while the titanuim armor floor kits helped reduce mine damage; however, the problems with

**During early field testing, factory representatives monitored the results and crew impressions. Early M551s did not have a standard grease fitting on the bogey wheels. Instead it had a small plug, into which oil was poured, situated behind the road wheel. A clear vision sight on the hub allowed the crew to monitor the oil level. A standard grease fittings was fitted to later vehicles. (Mihalenko)**

**This Sheridan of the 3/4th Cavalry is being returned to base on a low boy trailer after hitting a mine. The 3/4th Cavalry developed a dislike for the Sheridan after losing a number of vehicles to mines. The band around the barrel is in Red, identifying this Sheridan as belonging to A Troop. (Schimdt via Harlem)**

the electrical systems and combustible rounds were never satisfactorily solved. Numerous vehicles were so severely damaged by small mines that their crews considered them a total loss and destroyed the vehicles rather than attempting to retrieve them. Although the vehicle did achieve a certain degree of reliability as time progressed, its crews never fully trusted it. A great deal of this distrust was due to its inability to absorb battle damage, particularly an RPG hit. Such a hit usually completely destroyed the vehicle as a result of the secondary explosion of the main rounds. As a result of this, the crews quickly abandoned the vehicle when hit and often rode on top of the vehicle (except for the driver) for safety reasons. They would rely on personal weapons and/or the .50 caliber machine gun to engage the enemy.

As the U.S. wound down its commitment in Vietnam during the early 1970s, the Sheridans were some of the last armored vehicles to be withdrawn. Cavalry and armored units were kept in-country because of their firepower and mobility, as the infantry units were pulled out. Their last major action was during early 1971 when Sheridans supported ARVN forces engaged in Operation LAM SON 719. By the end of 1971, however, the remaining Sheridans had been packed up and shipped home for reconditioning and reissue to stateside and Europeans units.

In retrospect, the Sheridan's commitment to Vietnam was probably ill-advised. Designed for a European type conflict, it was not suited for the guerrilla style war waged in the jungles of Vietnam. In addition, its introduction into combat before the various bugs had been worked out hindered its effective employment. This hasty deployment was due almost entirely to the Army bureaucrats who needed to silence their critics about the way the Sheridan program had been handled.

Unfortunately, the ramifications of this decision would later haunt the Army as it tried to develop a new series of armored vehicles during the late 1970s and early 1980s. On the plus side, the Sheridan's service in Vietnam brought about numerous changes which were highlighted under actual combat conditions. These changes helped mold the vehicle into a more effective and reliable weapons system. Vietnam also showed the combat potential of the M551 and, although problems continued to plague it throughout the war, the Sheridan was shown to be a viable weapons system with a tremendous amount of firepower for a vehicle its size. While not the most effective weapon deployed to Vietnam by the Army, the Sheridan still managed to do an acceptable job — a reflection not only upon the vehicle, but on the American soldiers who crewed it.

One modification the Sheridan crews quickly made was to increase its external storage space. Field modifications included adding a larger rack to the turret and a jerry can rack fitted to the rear engine deck (although this was not done to all vehicles). These M-551s were assigned to the 11th ACR. (Squadron/Signal Archives)

Unusual things could and did happen in Vietnam. During a sweep near the Cambodian border, the crew of this Sheridan scared up a deer and shot it. The animal was flown back to the base camp, cleaned and butchered. When they returned, the men got a welcome change from their standard Army diet of C rations. (Mihalenko)

Both the M48 (left) and Sheridan (right) were damaged by land mines. While the Patton is relatively intact, the Sheridan's upper hull was separated from the lower hull by the mine blast and subsequent secondary internal explosion. It was unlikely that the vehicle was repaired, instead it was probably salvaged for parts. (USA)

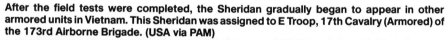

After the field tests were completed, the Sheridan gradually began to appear in other armored units in Vietnam. This Sheridan was assigned to E Troop, 17th Cavalry (Armored) of the 173rd Airborne Brigade. (USA via PAM)

The crew of this Sheridan, named *THE EXECUTIONER*, have rigged a poncho liner on top of the hull to provide some shade. The commander's position has been fitted with factory supplied armor shields for side protection and the crew has added an ACAV shield for frontal protection. (Mihalenko)

The crew of this Sheridan of the 1st Cavalry takes a break during jungle operations. The dense jungle made for ideal ambush conditions and the Sheridan's light armor provided little protection against Rocket Propelled Grenades (RPGs) and mines. Crews often abandoned their vehicles after being hit for fear of a secondary explosion. (USA via Armor)

One problem the Sheridan had was overheating in the hot, tropical climate. This was caused by faulty fan belts and weak pulleys. The crew of this tank performs preventive maintenance on the engine while in the field to avoid potential problems. (USA via Armor)

This Sheridan of the 11th ACR, in position along a trail near the Cambodian border, has been fitted with the supplemental bow armor as an added protection against land mines. The bolt on titanium armor helped lessen the effects of mines, but did not protect the vehicle completely. (Mihalenko)

In combat, sleep was precious and in Vietnam tank crews never got enough. During a lull in operations, these crewmen took the chance to grab a quick nap. This particular vehicle is fitted with the factory supplied armored shield at the back of the cupola and is piled high with extra gear. (USA via Armor)

A Sheridan is refueled from a tank truck during operations near Tam Ky in the early Spring of 1970. The commander's cupola is fitted with the factory designed gun shield which replaced the ACAV shield borrowed from M113 APCs. This vehicle belonged to A Troop, 1st Squadron, 1st Cavalry which was temporarily assigned to the Americal Division. (USA)

This M551 Sheridan of E Troop, 1st Cavalry, was operating just south of the DMZ on a search and clear mission during 1971. The extra gear stored on the turret was typical of the way most Sheridans looked in the field. Numerous names, graffiti and cartoon characters were also common on vehicles in Vietnam. (USA)

## Combat Modifications

**M551 (Early)**

- Unshielded Commander's .50 Caliber Machine Gun
- Open Breech Scavenger Gun Tube

**M551 (Vietnam)**

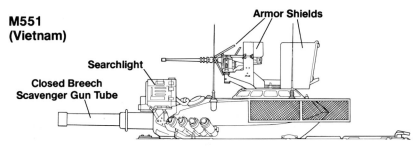

- Armor Shields
- Searchlight
- Closed Breech Scavenger Gun Tube

Logistics was an important part of the American war effort in Vietnam and Sheridans were often used to provide protection for supply convoys. This tank is helping tow a truck, loaded with artillery ammunition, up a hill near Khe Sanh during Operation DEWEY CANYON II. The sandbags on the hull top were extra protection for the driver. (USA)

The Cambodian incursion made use of nearly all of the armored units in the southern part of South Vietnam. Infantry from the 25th Division hitch a ride on this Sheridan during the invasion. The round objects below the turret are smoke grenade launchers, all of which have been apparently fired. (USA)

A Sheridan provides support for engineers during the closing days of American operations in Quang Ngai Province. The Sheridan never really used its amphibious capabilities in Vietnam and the "surfboard" on the front hull was often removed or lost during field operations. This tank is from E Troop, 1st Cavalry. (USA)

This Sheridan crew and their infantry escort relax for a moment during the Cambodian invasion. This M551 has been fitted with additional bow armor bolted to the lower part of the front hull. Constant operations in the field have either obliterated the vehicle markings or covered them with a thick coat of Red dirt. (USA)

Sheridans usually worked with the M113 ACAV Armored Personnel Carriers (APCs) during sweeps. These vehicles of the 2nd Battalion, 47th Infantry (Mechanized) took part in a sweep in Cambodia during the May 1970 invasion. This action sparked widespread anti-war demonstrations at colleges across the U.S. (USA)

This Sheridan is almost hidden by the gear carried on its hull and turret during operations in Cambodia. The object on the rear of the hull is a tow bar used to help recover damaged vehicles. The rubber on the road wheels has been chipped and worn down by constant use. The flag on the hull is Red and White with all numbers and letters in White. (USA)

A Sheridan of the 2nd Squadron, 11thACR rests behind a dirt birm at fire support base (FSB) Fiddler Green. This Sheridan has been modified with an extra machine gun in front of the loader's hatch to increase the vehicle's close in defensive firepower. (U.S. Army)

A Sheridan moves through a rubber plantation while on patrol near the Cambodian border during the Spring of 1970. The vehicle was assigned to C Troop, 1st Squadron, 11th ACR. (U.S. Army)

An early production M551 Sheridan of the Armor School at Fort Knox. These vehicles were used for training during the Fall of 1968.

This Sheridan of the 2nd Platoon, 1st Squadron, 11th ACR was used along the Cambodian border during 1969. It was common for Sheridans to carry more than one name in Vietnam.

*HARD CORE 7* was a Sheridan of B Troop, 3/4 Cavalry assigned to the 25th Infantry Division at Tay Nihn during February 1969.

Sheridans of the 1st Squadron, 116th Armored Cavalry Regiment, Idaho National Guard carried a desert type camouflage during the 1970s.

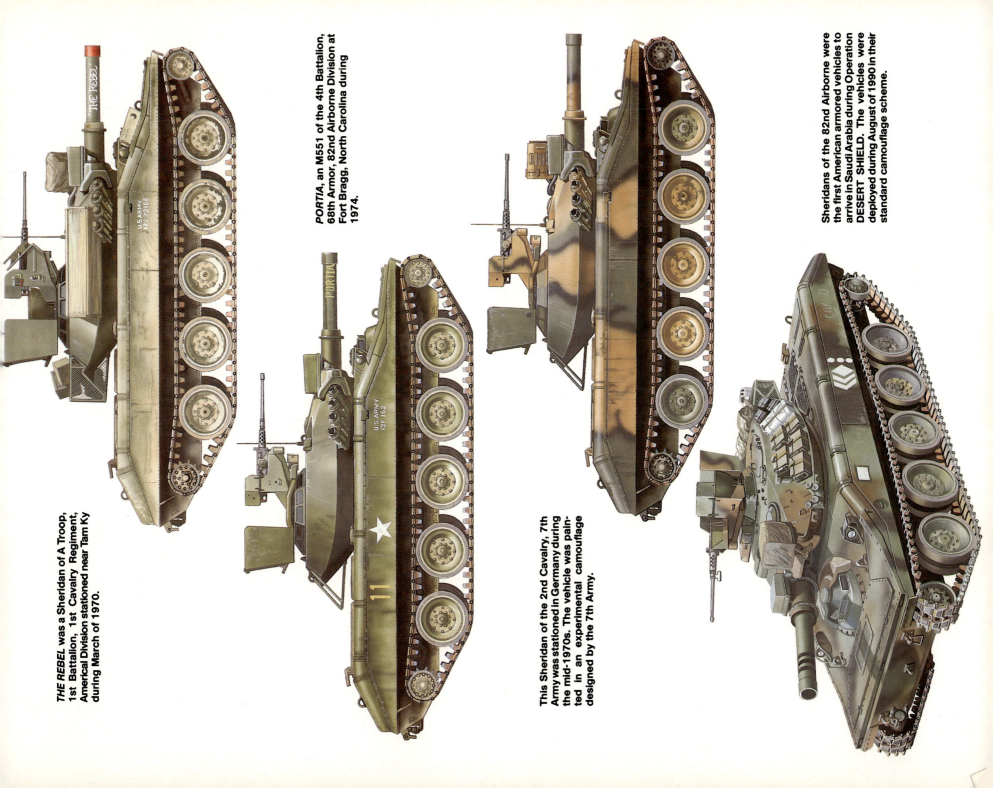

THE REBEL was a Sheridan of A Troop, 1st Battalion, 1st Cavalry Regiment, Americal Division stationed near Tam Ky during March of 1970.

PORTIA, an M551 of the 4th Battalion, 68th Armor, 82nd Airborne Division at Fort Bragg, North Carolina during 1974.

This Sheridan of the 2nd Cavalry, 7th Army was stationed in Germany during the mid-1970s. The vehicle was painted in an experimental camouflage designed by the 7th Army.

Sheridans of the 82nd Airborne were the first American armored vehicles to arrive in Saudi Arabia during Operation DESERT SHIELD. The vehicles were deployed during August of 1990 in their standard camouflage scheme.

# Post-Vietnam Service

Following the American withdrawal from Vietnam, the Sheridan continued to see service with various cavalry, armored and airborne units in the Army, National Guard and Army Reserve. Lessons learned from Vietnam led to a number modifications being made to the M551s that remained in service. During 1971, Hughes Aircraft produced the AN/VVG-1 Laser range finder for installation on the Sheridan. This system, comprised of a Ruby laser, optics and associated hardware was retrofitted to a number of vehicles and allowed the tank commander to acquire accurate target and range information within seconds. The range finder was mounted on the front of the Tank Commander's cupola under the .50 caliber machine gun mounting. Sheridans with this modification were designated as the M551A.

Additionally, vehicles assigned to the 82nd Airborne during the late 1980 were modified with different smoke grenade launchers. The earlier in-line mounting with four individual launcher tubes was changed to a single mounting containing four tubes in an over/under side-by-side arrangement. The mount was located in the same position as the earlier tubes and many vehicles still retain the mounts for the earlier style launchers.

During its production run some 1,700 Sheridans were produced and, of these, approximately one hundred were lost in Vietnam. This left some 1,600 vehicles available for use by the Army. The various problems associated with the gun and ammunition, however, proved to be a maintenance nightmare and, during 1978, the Army decided to phase out most of the Sheridans still in service, placing many vehicles in long term storage

A small number of Sheridans were assigned to a National Guard unit, while the 82nd Airborne Division retained their Sheridans to provide armor support in the event the Division was deployed. In addition, a large number of Sheridans were modified to look like various Soviet vehicles for use by resident units at the National Training Center located at Fort Irwin, California and the armor training command at Fort Knox, Kentucky. There was some talk of selling the remaining Sheridans to South Korea (for a low price) where they might be rearmed with a more conventional armament, but this never came to pass.

## Panama

Aside from field maneuvers, the Sheridan has only been used in combat once since Vietnam. This occurred during December of 1989, when the United States carried out Operation JUST CAUSE, which was designed to oust Panamanian strongman Manuel Noriega.

The Sheridans were used in Panama for several reasons. They were organic to the 82nd Airborne, they were more easily deployed than the M1 Abrams, they were better suited to the city streets and narrow roads in Panama and the Panamanians had no armored vehicles which could seriously challenge the Sheridan.

This operation served to highlight the need for a modern lightweight armored vehicle for use by the airborne forces to replace the aging Sheridan. The replacement has yet to come about and the Sheridans of the 82nd Airborne were once again deployed, this time half a world away from their base in the U.S.

## Saudi Arabia

On 2 August 1990, the Iraqi President Saddam Hussein launched an invasion of his neighbor to the south, Kuwait. On 8 August, President George Bush of the United States called for an international military force to both protect Saudi Arabia from an Iraqi invasion and to oust Iraq from Kuwait. This operation quickly became known around the world as Operation DESERT SHIELD.

Within six days of the Iraqi invasion, a reinforced brigade of the 82nd Airborne, once again including their M551 Sheridans, had been deployed by USAF C-141 and C-5 aircraft to Saudi Arabia. The Sheridans were some of the first American armored vehicles to arrive in the Kingdom. The Sheridan remained the principal U.S. armored vehicle in the area until joined, during late August, by USMC M60 MBTs and M1 Abrams MBTs of the 2nd Armored Divison and 1st Cavalry Division.

**Following the American withdrawal from Vietnam the Army shifted its focus to Europe and built up its units. A number of cavalry units were re-equipped with the Sheridan and the vehicle became a common sight in Germany. These Sheridans of the 1st Cavalry move down a German road during one of the annual REFORGER exercises. (USA)**

As part of the strategy to defend Europe a great deal of equipment was pre-positioned, requiring only troops to man them. These M551s of the 3rd Cavalry are in a storage depot awaiting the arrival of troops during REFORGER 77. They are fitted with the late style armor shields around the commander's .50 caliber machine gun. (USA)

*Chicanos Can*, a Sheridan of an unidentified Cavalry unit, moves along the side of a canal in Germany during war games. Such personal markings were unofficial and more often than not were highly discouraged by higher headquarters. (USA via Armor)

Two Sheridans of the 2/4th Cavalry, 4th Armored Division maneuver along a road in Germany. During the early 1970s vehicles were still painted basic Olive Drab; however, during the mid-1970s the 7th Army began to experiment with various camouflaged patterns. (USA via Armor)

*BARE-FOOT* lacks the armored commanders cupola and four-in-a-row grenade launchers. In their place, the crew has added a jerry can and extra track links stored on the turret. (USA via Armor)

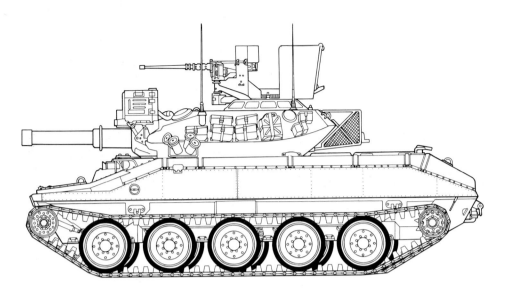
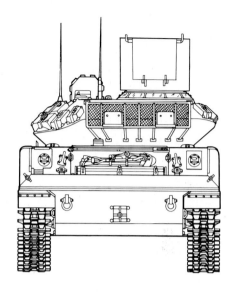

## Specifications

## M551A Sheridan

| | |
|---|---|
| **Crew** | Four |
| **Length** | 20.43 Feet |
| **Width** | 9.25 Feet |
| **Height** | 9.66 Feet |
| **Weight** | 34,899 pounds |

| | |
|---|---|
| **Armament** | |
| Main | 152MM gun/missile launcher. |
| Secondary | One 7.62MM coaxial machine gun. One .50 caliber M2 Browning on commander's coupla. |
| **Engine** | Detroit-Diesel 6V-53T 300 hp turbocharged diesel engine. |
| **Speed** | 43.5 mph |
| **Range** | 373 miles |

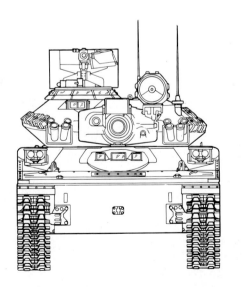
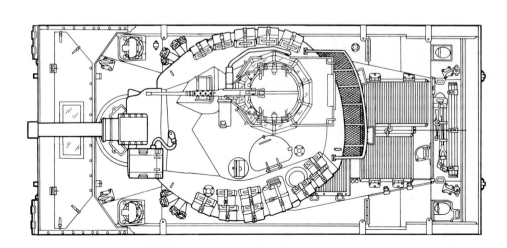

This Sheridan has been painted in a camouflage scheme devised by 7th Army. Numerous variations were tried and eventually these were replaced by official schemes developed by the Mobility Equipment Research and Development Command (MERDC) during the late 1970s. This vehicle is from the 2nd Cavalry, B Troop. (USA via Armor)

During war games curious civilians often watched the proceedings. Perhaps this German father remembered an earlier generation of U.S. tankers as he points out something on the tank to his children while members of the 2nd Cavalry work on their Sheridan. (USA via Armor)

To supplement the camouflage paint scheme on their Sheridan, these tankers have added vegetation to the turret and hull. This M551 was assigned to the 1st Infantry Division which had deployed to Europe for REFORGER 74. (USA)

In Germany the Sheridan was far more reliable than in Vietnam since maintenance facilities were better and more numerous. The missile system and combustible rounds, however, still caused problems. These problems led to an Army decision to retire both the Sheridan and the M60A2. (USA)

Painted in the MERDC camouflage scheme, this Sheridan took part in a training exercise in the U.S. The round object above the first bogey wheel is the recess for an exterior activated fire extinguisher which, when pulled, would douse an engine compartment fire. (USA via Armor)

The crew of this Sheridan takes a break during a training exercise at the National Training Center during the late 1970s. The tank has been given a rough camouflage scheme of Green, Brown and Light Tan to help it blend in more with the surrounding terrain. (USA)

Numerous National Guard cavalry units were equipped with the Sheridan. This M551 of the Idaho National Guard took part in Summer camp training during the mid-1970s (prior to the introduction of standard camouflage schemes). It is assigned to the 116th Armored Cavalry Regiment.

The Sheridan was designed originally for use with airborne forces and continued to serve in that role even after having been withdrawn from regular service. This M551 teams up with a jeep mounted TOW unit. Such a combination provided a great deal of firepower and mobility for the airborne forces without seriously hampering their ability to deploy. (USA)

A pair of camouflaged M551As of the 82nd Airborne Division. The vehicle in the background is equipped with a laser range finder mounted under the .50 caliber machine gun on the commander's cupola. The armor shield on the front of the gun has been deleted. (82nd Airborne PAO)

An M551A Sheridan from the 3/73rd Armor of the 82nd Airborne Division on parade in the late 1980s. This unit had originally been the 4/64th Armor before being redesignated. The number 13 and pentagon on the hull sides are in Black. (82nd Airborne PAO)

## Laser Range Finder

**M551 (Early)**

**M551A**

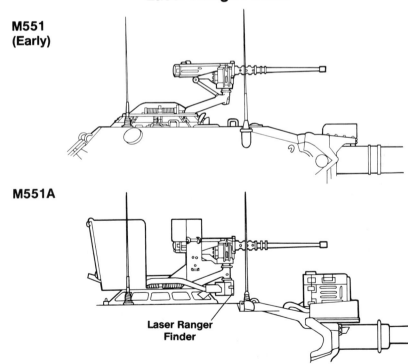

Laser Ranger Finder

The 82nd regularly deploys Sheridans to the NTC to take part in desert maneuvers. This vehicle is from Alpha Troop, 1st Platoon. The device on the main gun barrel is a gun fire blank simulator. (82nd Airborne PAO)

An M551A of the 82nd Airborne Division guards a road in Panama during Operation JUST CAUSE, the U.S. effort to oust GEN Manuel Noriega. (USA via Mike Green)

M551As of the 82nd Airborne Division shortly after their arrival in Saudi Arabia as part of Operation DESERT SHIELD. The Sheidans were the first American armored vehicles to arrive in the kingdom. (USA via Mike Green)

The driver of an 82nd Airborne Sheridan in the Saudi desert takes a long drink of cool water. Troops have been warned that the conditions in the desert make it necessary for them to consume large quanities of water to ward off the effects of heat stroke. (USA via Mike Green)

# OPFOR Sheridans

Following the withdrawal of he M551 from active duty, the Army decided to modify some 300 Sheridans to look like a variety of modern Soviet armored vehicles. These "Soviet" M551s were given a new outline by using a VISMOD (Visual Modification) kit of sheet metal, plywood and fiberglass. Once completed, the VISMOD Sheridans were used to simulate Soviet T-72 tanks, BMP Mechanized Infantry Combat Vehicles, ZSU-23-4 four barreled 23MM anti-aircraft vehicles and 122MM M-1974 self-propelled guns. Officially designated the M551A2, the majority of these VISMOD vehicles were assigned to the National Training Center (NTC) located at Fort Irwin, in the high desert of California.

At the NTC the VISMOD Sheridans were deployed along the lines of a Soviet Motor Rifle Regiment in simulated war games against visiting armored units. Closely following current Soviet tactical doctrine the Opposing Forces (OPFOR) troops, also known as the 32nd Guards Motorized Rifle Regiment, added a realism that had been previously missing from Army training. The maneuvers held in the hot California desert came as close to combat as you could in peacetime. This live training scenario, using Soviet tactics and equipment designed to simulated weapons currently in the Soviet inventory, came about due to the highly successful *Top Gun* and *Red Flag* exercises run by the Navy and the Air Force.

Basically each VISMOD Sheridan was reconfigured to look like the appropriate Russian vehicle using a VISMOD kit of sheet metal, fiberglass and plywood. In addition, all OPFOR M551s were fitted with the Multiple Integrated Laser Engagement System (MILES) and its associated hardware. Each vehicle was equipped with a laser "gun" to engage other MILES equipped vehicles and personnel. The whole system was tied to a computer on the tank which registered when another tank scored a "hit". This computer determines if the "hit" was a near miss, a disabling shot, or a kill and what weapon was used to score the hit. In the case of a "kill", a continuous tone is heard in the tank, a Yellow rotating strobe light is lit, smoke is emitted from the killed tank, the engine is shut down and the laser gun ceases to operate. All of this is tied to a main computer by microwave transmitters. This allows a compete record of the engagement to be recorded and later reviewed by those who took part in the battle.

The resident "Soviet" tankers of the 32nd Guards have acquired a well deserved reputation for excellence throughout the U.S. Army. Many visiting units, thinking that they would have an easy time at the desert facility, have been unpleasantly surprised by the losses they have taken at the hands of the OPFOR units. Using their intimate knowledge of the terrain and familiarity with their equipment, the OPFOR personnel have yet to lose a major engagement during training exercises at the NTC.

Besides the VISMOD vehicles, M551 Sheridans are also used by the Observer/Controllers (OCs), the umpires of the wargames. These vehicles have had much of their armor removed and are equipped with extra communications equipment and a "God Gun," a MILES laser gun used to disable vehicles from either side that have been destroyed by mines, artillery or other means. Most OC vehicles are overall Desert Sand in color.

The realism with the VISMOD vehicles and the simulated battlefield conditions at Fort Irwin have brought the Army tactical training syllabus into the modern era and have resulted in far reaching benefits. Units which have taken part in maneuvers at Fort Irwin, which normally last three weeks, have gained a new understanding of armored combat in the harsh terrain and climate at the base, while sharpening their combat skills against an opponent well versed in modern armor tactics. GEN George Patton's famous quote, "the more you sweat in peace, the less you bleed in war," can find no better example than at the NTC today.

Following the success of the highly realistic Navy Top Gun and Air Force Red Flag programs, the Army decided to make its training more realistic. In order to provide visual realism it was decided to modify several hundred Sheridans to look like Soviet vehicles. This Sheridan, from the Armor School at Fort Knox, has been modified to look like a T-72 MBT. (Mesko)

This Sheridan, with its gun/missile launcher barrel removed, has been reconfigured to resembled a Soviet BMP armored personnel carrier. Both this vehicle and the T-72 are painted Field Green for use at Fort Knox. (Mesko)

The main location for the VISMOD Sheridans is the National Training Center (NTC) at Fort Irwin, California. This VISMOD Sheridan carries a two tone camouflage scheme and is configured to look like a Soviet 122mm Self-Propelled Howitzer. (USA via PAM)

The final Sheridan VISMOD AFV in the inventory is the ZSU-23-4 anti-aircraft gun platform, complete with a non-operating radar dish. All of the vehicles are fitted with laser guns which are tied into the MILES training system's onboard sensors and computers. (USA via PAM)

## Soviet Armor

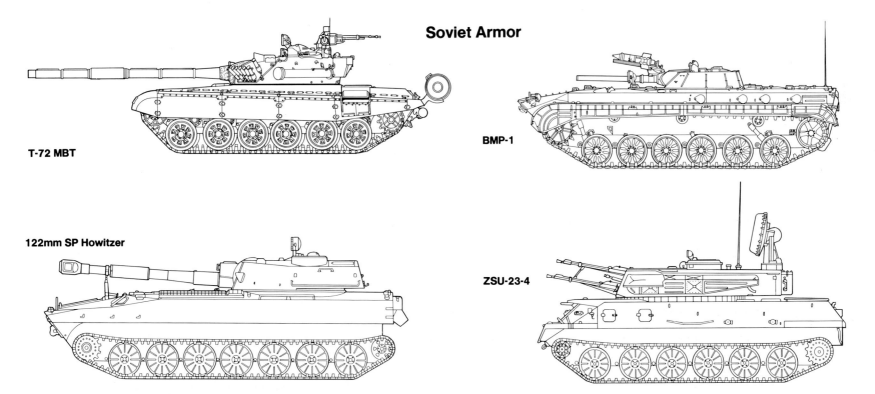

T-72 MBT

BMP-1

122mm SP Howitzer

ZSU-23-4

35

Because of the Sheridan's angular hull, fenders are added to the sides to make it look more like the Soviet vehicle it is intended to simulate (like this VISMOD T-72). (Mesko)

The main modification to all the vehicles is a turret and fittings made from fiberglass, wood and sheet metal which fits over the Sheridan turret. Cutouts are made for the hatches and various sights on the turret roof of this VISMOD T-72. (Mesko)

The gun tubes of the OPFOR Soviet look alike vehicles are made from thin sheet metal and are attached to the Sheridan's gun/missile launcher barrel (except in the case of the BMP). (Green)

Each vehicle is different in style. Besides the turrets, the front decking of the VISMOD T-72 is different from the front decking of the VISMOD ZSU-23-4. The cutouts on each fender addition are to give the driver limited side vision which would be completely blocked if the fenders were solid. (Green)

Realism is the key to the success achieved at the NTC, with the enemy troops copying Russian tactics, uniforms and combat techniques, including the use of signal flags. The rail above the "gun" tube on this VISMOD BMP normally carries a dummy Sagger anti-tank guided missile fitted to it. (Green)

## Specialized Training Equipment

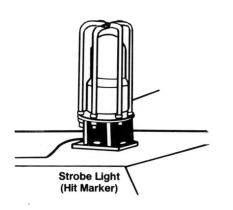

Strobe Light (Hit Marker)

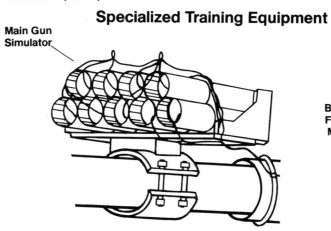

Main Gun Simulator

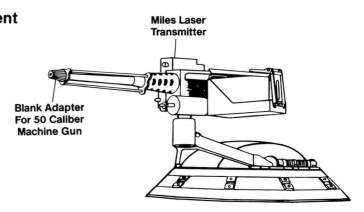

Miles Laser Transmitter

Blank Adapter For 50 Caliber Machine Gun

Two VISMOD BMPs lead a charge against an opponent as a VISMOD T-72 moves up in the background. Many visiting units come to the NTC thinking that it will be a "piece of cake", but after their first encounter with the OPFOR group they quickly learn how mistaken they are. (Green)

While these Sheridans would never fool anyone closeup, at a distance they do look like the real thing. These vehicles are forming for an "attack" against a visiting Army armor unit. Included in the "Soviet" formation are several MT-LBs for added realism. (USA via PAM)

The Sheridan's performance allows it to move at a high rate of speed, making it a difficult target to hit. The MILES laser detector strips are installed around the bottom of the turret. Just behind the gun barrel is a gunfire simulator while the commander's .50 caliber machine gun is fitted with a blank fire adapter which shreds the wooden rounds. (Green)

(Above)
A column of VISMOD T-72s traverse their turrets toward an approaching threat. Under such hazy/dusty conditions, the VISMOD Sheridans do look like their Soviet counterparts and give the training at the NTC the realism required. Never before has the Army provided conditions as close to the real battlefield and the benefits gained by the units taking part in the training are tremendous. (Green)

(Below)
The crew of this VISMOD BMP scans the horizon in search of enemy vehicles. The AT-3 Sagger anti-tank missile is mounted above the gun barrel. The small light just behind it is a beacon used to signal when the vehicle is disabled. It will flash and a smoke grenade will go off if the vehicle is "killed" in action. (Green)

# M551 Variants

Aside from its use by the OPFOR at the NTC, the M551 was involved in a number of test projects to see if other uses could be found for the vehicle. The majority of the 1,500 tanks currently in storage have relatively little mileage on them and are mechanically sound, making them attractive as the possible basis for new vehicles.

## ARMVAL

During the late 1970s, the Army and Marine Corps began to look for a lightweight armored vehicle, capable being airlifted by cargo aircraft or helicopter. This vehicle was intended to be used by quick reaction forces. During the Fall of 1978, ten M551s were modified for testing in the Advanced Anti-Armor Vehicle Evaluation (ARMVAL) program. These vehicles were sent to the Tank Automotive Research and Development Command plant at Warren, Michigan, where they were extensively modified for use in the project.

At the plant, the vehicles had some of their armor and the main armament removed to lighten them. In addition, their old engines were replaced by the same engine used in the Marine Corps LVTP-7 (uprated for a higher power-to-weight ratio). To improve cross country performance, changes were made in the suspension and, with the anticipation that a prime area of employment would be in the Middle East, a new powerplant cooling system was installed. With less weight and more power, the speed of modified M551s rose slightly, from 42 miles an hour to 44 mph.

In place of the 152MM gun/missile launcher, a laser gun set to simulate a 75MM cannon was installed. A West German Staget sighting system was installed along with a modified M36E2 optical sight as a backup for the gunner. The tank commander could also use the Staget system along with a backup M20A3 daylight optical sight.

A great deal of useful information was obtained from the test program using the modified M551s. While no new production vehicles resulted from this project, the data gathered was used on other vehicles which were under development and work continues in an attempt to find a lightweight air transportable AFV which can carry an armament capable of dealing with heavier main battle tanks.

## 75MM ARES Kenetic Energy Weapons Test Sheridan

A novel armament system was installed on an M551 which consisted of the 75MM ARES cannon in an elevating mount. This system replaced the standard turret and gun/missile launcher of the Sheridan. The ARES cannon, fed by a automatic loading system, is part of the Elevated Kinetic-Energy Weapons Task Program under testing by the Tank Automotive Research and Development Command.

The test bed consisted of an M551 with the turret removed and replaced by a new turret with the ARES 75MM gun. The cannon can be elevated from it resting position on top of the hull and receives its ammunition via an elevator tube from a storage carousal mounted within the small turret. The gun is stabilized in elevation and the turret is stabilized in azimuth. When the cannon is fired from a lowered position a specially modified M36 sight is used. If the gun is fired from the elevated position, the current Improved TOW sighting system is employed for locating and acquiring target information.

While this is purely a research project with no plans for rearming the remaining Sheridans, a wealth of information has been gathered. Data from using the elevated gun mount has led to changes to improve its reliability. Information obtained during testing has also been used in the Rapid Deployment Force Light Tank (RDFLT) project. It is unknown if such a vehicle will ever go into production; however, research with the vehicle continues in order to mate technological advances with a practical vehicle capable of employment.

## Other Variants

Originally, the Sheridan was to have served as the basis for a number of other vehicles. These included two anti-aircraft variants (equipped with either missiles or guns), support vehicles, a 155MM self-propelled gun, an APC, a mortar carrier, engineer versions, and a bridge layer. Although some of these reached the mock-up stage, or possibly even a prototype, the problems with the Sheridan's development and a cut in funding by Congress eventually led to the cancellation of these various projects.

**Ten Sheridans were modified for use in the Advanced Anti-Armor Vehicle Examination during the late 1970s. Their armament was removed, along with some armor. These special vehicles were used to evaluate a new power plant, suspension components and various optics/sighting systems. Data obtained from this program was used by the Army and Marine Corps toward development of a new generation of light armored vehicles. (PAM)**

This Sheridan has been modified with an unmanned turret, armed with a 75mm ARES gun to test the viability of this armament. The configuration lowered the basic weight of the vehicle and cut down on the number of crewmen (due to a powered ammunition feed system). The elevating gun mount allowed the Sheridan to use terrain features to the best possible advantage by raising the gun from cover while the tank remained concealed. (PAM)

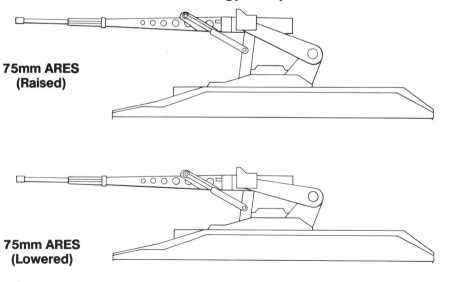

### Elevated Kinetic Energy Weapon Test Bed

**75mm ARES (Raised)**

**75mm ARES (Lowered)**

This experimental Sheridan was fitted with a 105mm cannon; however, the weapon proved to be too heavy and powerful for the light hull. Trials were held with and without a muzzle brake fitted, but there was little difference between the two. The various markings on the hull and gun are reference points for cameras filming the firing tests. (PAM)

This Sheridan was armed with a specially designed 105mm gun and turret equipped with a soft recoil system. The turret was jointly developed by Cadillac Gage and Royal Ordnance of England. This turret was later used on the Cadillac Gage Commando Stingray light tank. (PAM)

Some Sheridans used at the NTC were converted for use as umpire vehicles. These vehicles have their guns removed and special equipment is installed to allow them to monitor engagements between the opposing forces. (USA)

These modified Sheridans gave the umpires greater protection and mobility then the Hummers and jeeps normally used in war games. While these Sheridans are painted Olive Drab, current ones have received a camouflage Desert Sand to help cut down on the heat from the hot desert sun. (USA via Armor)

A number of Sheridans were stripped of their turrets and fitted with a variety of specialized equipment that was undergoing testing, such as this vehicle. All markings on the hull are in White. (PAM)

# A Replacement Vehicle

During the 1970s American defense strategy shifted. While Europe was still considered critical, the importance of the Middle East and its vital oil fields took on a new importance. In order to protect U.S. interests in this area, the Pentagon developed the Rapid Deployment Force (RDF). This force was designed for rapid insertion into the area in case of internal trouble or outside aggression. The need for a lightweight armored vehicle with heavy enough armament to provide a degree of protection against enemy armor soon became highly evident. As a result, the Army expressed an interest to the armament industry for such a vehicle to replace the aging Sheridan in this role.

## HSTV-L

The first vehicle developed was the High Survivability Test Vehicle - Lightweight (HSTV-L). This vehicle was developed under the direction of the Tank Automotive Command (TACOM) and was a testbed to be used in experiments with a variety of different equipment such as stabilization, fire control and electronics. Developed by the AAI Corporation in Maryland, the HSTV-L was armed with a 75MM ARES automatic smoothbore cannon and carried a crew of three.

For close in defense the vehicle was equipped with an M240 7.62 MM machine mounted coaxial to the main gun on the starboard side and another M240 7.62 MM machine gun mounted on the commanders coupla. Smoke grenade launchers were fitted to both sides of the turret.

The HSTV-L used a radical new sighting system known as the hunter/killer sight. The sight is independent of the turret and can be rotated while the turret remains stationary. Once a target was identified, the sight is shifted to the killer mode and the turret is aligned with it. While the gunner engages the target, the tank commander can continuing hunting for new targets with his sight. The system also has Forward Looking Infrared (FLIR) optics for both the commander and gunner.

Besides the sights, the digital fire control system receives inputs from various sensors including a cross wind sensor, muzzle reference sensor and an eye-safe laser range finder. The fully stabilized system is capable of fire on the move with a high probability of a first round hit. The fire control system allows any crew member to fire the weapons.

Essentially a test vehicle, the HSTV-L was used to try out various concepts regarding lightweight armored vehicles. Initial testing began during 1982 and continued into the latter part of the decade.

## Rapid Deployment Force Light Tank

The AAL Corporation followed the HSTV-L with a private venture light tank of their own design, the Rapid Deployment Force Light Tank (RDT/LT) during late 1980. Based on the HSTV-L, the new vehicle was also armed with the 75MM ARES cannon. This gun, fed from a automatic magazine containing sixty rounds, could fire one shell a second and was housed in a one man turret manned by the commander. The other two crewmen, a driver and gunner, were seated forward of the turret, each with his own hatch.

The High Survivability Test Vehicle (Light Weight) was essentially an experimental armored vehicle built to test certain items of equipment. Designed under the direction of TACOM by AAI, the HSTV-L allowed the Army to try various systems and arrangements without spending a large amount of money on prototypes. At the same time, these tests layed the foundation for a possible Sheridan replacement. (PAM)

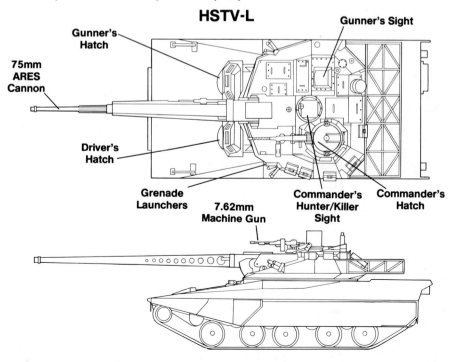

Using their experience with the HSTV-L, AAI developed their own light tank for possible sale at home and abroad. The initial vehicle mounted a 75MM ARES cannon in a one man turret. The gun has a maximum elevation of 40° giving the tank a limited anti-aircraft capability when using canister or high explosive rounds with proximity fuses. (AAI)

The 75MM ARES cannon gave the vehicle a lethal punch. Its high rate of fire and high muzzle velocity provided sufficient firepower without imposing a heavy weight penalty. Capable of firing armor piercing, high explosive, fragmentation, and canister rounds, the gun had a 40° elevation which gave it a limited anti-aircraft capability. The high rate of fire allowed the gun to hit the same area of an opposing tank numerous times, shattering the heavier armor associated with main battle tanks.

Mounted above and behind the main gun is a stabilized rotary primary sight head. The fire control system is fully stabilized and is tied into an onboard fire control digital computer. The RDF/LT uses the same hunter/killer sighting system first tested on the HSTV-L.

The RDF/LT has an all-welded aluminum armor hull with separate hatches for the gunner and driver. Between them is mounted an auxiliary sight for the main armament. Besides the 75MM cannon the vehicle is armed with a coaxial 7.62MM machine gun carried on the starboard side of the main gun. For increased protection, provision has been made for mounting applique armor to the hull.

While this vehicle was being developed, AAL also decided to design a lighter version with a two man crew, with the gun being housed in an unmanned turret. Other than its lower weight and new turret, the two vehicles are identical. The commander was seated to the right of the driver and used a roof mounted sight to control the gun.

While work proceeded on the RDF/LT, AAL developed another turret equipped with a 76MM cannon for foreign customers (the 75mm ARES cannon was not cleared for export). The armament consisted of an M32 gun, the same as used in the M41 Walker Bulldog light tank (which was still in service throughout the world). The two man turret was considerable different than the earlier turrets and, although the same chassis was used, the production version was slated to be slightly revised. New ammunition, developed by AAL from experience gained working with the 75MM ARES ammunition gave the old 76MM cannon a far better chance of destroying current Russian armor.

**AAI's second version of the light tank, had the cannon mounted in an unmanned turret which resulted in the crew being reduced to two men. Both versions were equipped with a nine-round computer controlled automatic loading system. (AAI)**

The 76mm gun armed RDF/LT undergoes field trials. The legend on the hull side reads U.S. Army/U.S. Marine Corps, identifying the program as a joint effort to find a vehicle capable of meeting both Army and Marine requirements. (AAI)

A third version was developed for export sales since the ARES cannon was not cleared for overseas sale. The M32 76mm cannon used in the M41 Walker Bulldog light tank was substituted in a new turret with new ammunition for the gun which raised the probability of a kill. Although the turret was mounted on the original chassis, the production version was to have a slightly revised hull. (AAI)

The ARES gun armed RDF/LT was capable of being air lifted by Lockheed C-5 (eight tanks), Lockheed C-141 (two tanks) and Lockheed C-130 (one tank) transports. The Low Altitude Parachute Extraction System was envisioned to be the most common method of combat deployment. (AAI)

# Armored Gun System Vehicles

While AAI was working on this series of light tanks, the Army decided (based on intelligence reports) that the new generation of Soviet armor would be able to resist the 75MM ARES armament due to advances in armor and design. As a result of this information the Army concluded that the smallest armament capable of dealing with these new Russian tanks was the 105MM gun. With this in mind, the Army, during 1981, stated their requirements for a new Armored Gun System (AGS) program designed to provide an armored vehicle for the RDF and to supplement existing armored forces. One goal of the project was to use as many "off-the-shelf" components as possible to cut down cost and development time. Additionally, the requirement states that the vehicle has armor protection and mobility equal to or better than the Sheridan.

Three companies eventually developed vehicles based on the AGS requirement. The most conventional of the three was the one designed by Cadillac Gage in Michigan. Nicknamed the "Commando Stingray," the light tank mounted a unique soft recoil L-7 105MM gun and a turret designed jointly with Royal Ordnance of England. Overall weight was kept down in the chassis by the use of high hardness Cadloy armor which provided good ballistic protection, particularly in combination with the angular design of the "Stingray." The low silhouette of the vehicle and its small size in comparison to other tanks also allowed it to be easily concealed. As the design was developed, it increased in weight to the point that it is no longer capable of being air-dropped. Although out of the running for the AGS program, the Stingray has been purchased by the Royal Thai Army.

The second entry, designed by FMC was the Close Combat Vehicle, Light (CCVL) using components from the M113 and M2/M3 Bradley. Outwardly the CCVL followed conventional tank design, but inside the crew was reduced to three through the use of an automatic loader, developed by FMC's Northern Ordnance Division. This auto loader could fire twelve 105MM rounds a minute, although it currently was limited to ten rounds per minute. Using similar sighting equipment to that installed on the M1 Abrams, the CCVL could engage targets under all kinds of weather and battlefield conditions. Ballistic protection was based on a form of laminated armor, similar to that found on the Bradley Infantry Fighting Vehicle, and protected against 30MM fire over a frontal arc of 60°, while the rest of the tank could resist heavy machine gun fire. On 10 July 1990 the vehicle was demonstrated to the Army at Fort Bragg, North Carolinia. The vehicle was tested alongside a Sheridan and a Marine Corps LAV-25. Additionally, a new vehicle based on the CCVL is being developed by FMC for the export market, this vehicle has a number of changes and is currently designated the VFM-5.

The last vehicle, produced by Teledyne Continatel Motors, mounted a 105MM cannon in an unmanned mount carried far back on the hull. This was the most unconventional of the three vehicles and had its engine mounted in front. Like the CCVL, the vehicle had an autoloading system using a computer controlled nine round ammunition drum. An additional thirty-three rounds was carried in ready and stowed positions within the hull. The low profile hull, with the engine up front provided good protection for the crew. Teledyne has devised a series of associated armament packs to go with the vehicles, including a 120MM gun turret, an APC version and an air defense variant.

While these vehicles are under consideration at the present, the Army has yet to issue an official list of requirements for the AGS vehicle. Budgetary restrictions and the lessening of tensions with the Soviet Union has not helped gain Congressional support for the project. While many advances have been made in light tank technology, the entire program may be shelved if the Army cannot convince Congress of a need for such a vehicle.

Ironically the use of the Sheridan in Panama and Saudi Arabia may rekindle interest in these projects. The need for such a vehicle is evident in light of the United States continued commitments around the world, particularly in the Middle East and other Third World countries.

Changing requirements eventually led the Army to specify that the minimum gun needed to defeat the latest generation of Soviet armor would have to be at least a 105MM. Cadillac Gage developed their entry into the competition, named the Stingray. Using the tried and proven L-7 105MM cannon, they developed (in conjunction with Royal Ordinance) a new recoil system to allow the weapon to be carried on a light chassis. (Cadillac Gage)

Although too heavy to meet the parachute drop requirement of the AGS program, the Stingray light tank has been adopted for service by the Royal Thai Army. (Mike Green)

FMC also entered the competition with a vehicle using M113 and M2/M3 Bradley components under the designation Close Combat Vehicle, Light (CCVL). To cut down on the crew size, the vehicle was equipped with an automatic loader developed by FMC for use with the 105MM L-7 cannon. (Green)

The CCVL light tanks carries an L-7 105MM cannon and thirty-two smoke grenade launchers arranged in banks of sixteen on each side of the turret. The vehicle uses many of the same sighting/optical systems as does the M1 Abrams MBT. (Mike Green)

The CCVL is not much taller than an M113 Armored Personnel Carrier (also produced by FMC). To lessen its recoil, the main gun has a multi-port muzzle break. The device on top of the muzzle is the muzzle reference sensor. (Mike Green)

The hull of the CCVL has a lot in common with the M2/M3 Bradley series of armored vehicles. The armor is designed to protect the crew from up to 14.5MM rounds and shell fragments. With modular applique armor, the protection is raised to 30MM. (Mike Green)

One of the CCVL test vehicles undergoing field trials. The vehicle is fast enough to keep up with both the M1 Abrams and M2/M3 Bradley. The need for a new armored vehicle for the Rapid Deployment Forces has been most recently demonstrated by the deployment of 82nd Airborne Sheridans to Saudi Arabia. (Mike Green)

The most radical design to enter the AGS competition was from Teledyne which featured a front mounted engine and a 105MM L-7 gun carried in an unmanned turret mounted toward the rear of the hull. The slopped hull and front mounted engine gave good forward protection for the crew. (Green)

The low overall height of the Teledyne AGS light tank would give the vehicle a decided tactical advantage. The unmanned turret features an auto loading 105MM L-7 cannon. The machine gun alongside the main weapon is an M60 7.62MM machine gun. (Mike Green)

When compared to a standard medium tank, the small size and low height of the Teledyne light tank's unmanned turret is evident. This vehicle was the most unconventional of the designs under consideration for the AGS program. (Mike Green)

This vehicle is a follow-on design based on FMC's Close Combat Vehicle Light (CCVL). The light tank is developed for the export market under the designation VFM-5. (Mike Green).

# U. S. ARMY ARMOR IN ACTION

2016

2025

2023

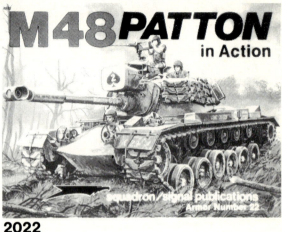

2022

2026

 squadron/signal publications